THE KIDS DO IT BOOK

THE KIDS DO IT BOOK

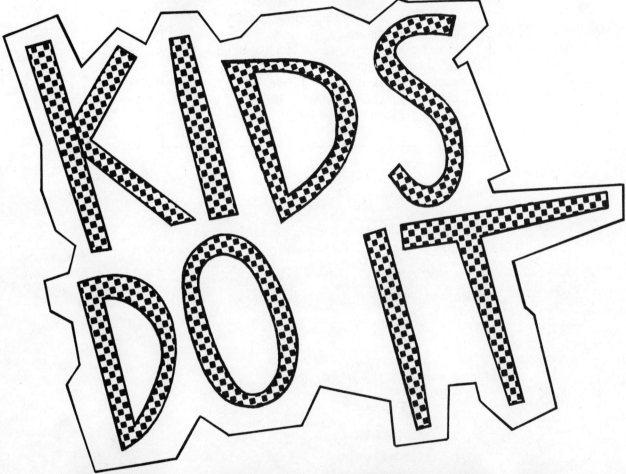

written by Paula Jorde   illustrations by Dennis Lee

Glide

Jorde, Paula.
    The kids do it book.

    Published in 1973 under title: Living &
learning with children.
    1. Education, Preschool—Handbooks, manuals,
etc. 2. Creative activities and seat work—Handbooks,
manuals, etc. I. Lee, Dennis. II. Title.
LB1140.2.J67 1976   649'.5   76-796
ISBN 0-912078-47-2

The **Kids Do It Book** is a revised, expanded and updated edition
of *Living and Learning With Children* (copyright ©1973 by Paula Jorde).

Order directly from:

> Glide Publications
> 330 Ellis Street
> San Francisco, California 94102
>
> $3.95 paperback
> please add $.50 for postage and handling

Design: Joel Goldstein
Composition: Zoe Brown
Production: Charlsen + Johansen & Others

CONTENTS

Dear Parent,

You are your child's most important teacher. During the first five years of life, your role in shaping your child's intellectual and emotional development is crucial. The learning experiences that s/he encounters in the family home during this period will later have a great impact on his or her success in school. In a sense, however, your task as a teacher is an easy one. Young children are eager and anxious to learn. Their natural sense of curiosity drives them to question, explore and discover more about the world in which they live. You have probably been amazed (and at times annoyed) with your child's unending search for answers. But this desire to understand and the ability to absorb each new experience is what motivates a child to search out and learn more about life. What children need, though, is direction and guidance. This is where your relationship with your child is vital. S/he looks to you as a vital source of knowledge and help. **The Kids Do It Book** was written for this reason. The activities on the following pages are designed to help you help your child become a successful learner.

Because you know your child better than anyone else, it is up to you to select activities that are appropriate to your child's age and ability level. In other words, use your judgment in selecting activities that will not pressure or frustrate him or her, yet will encourage thinking and learning. The wording you use to present an activity is also very important and should vary, of course, according to your child's age and ability.

You will notice that all measurements in **The Kids Do It Book** are given in metric. I hope that as you do the activities with your child you will use metric measurements exclusively. Don't clutter your child's mind with the English equivalents. These are intended only to assist you in converting to the new system. Our goal is to have children begin to Think Metric starting with their earliest experiences with measurement activities.

When playing some of the learning games in this handbook, keep in mind the following points:

Be Patient. Children need a lot of time to think. When they are pressured to hurry up or perform faster, the game will no longer be fun. Try to avoid giving hints or answers; let your child learn to think independently. If s/he makes a mistake, don't make a big deal out of it. Let your child know that learning involves making mistakes and encourage another try. Avoid creating a teacher-student relationship. Dig in and try some of these games and activities yourself—you'll be surprised what fun it can be to fingerpaint and color again.

Praise, Praise, Praise. Recognize your child's accomplishments, no matter how small. Select games that will build confidence and bring success. Remember, *children are not motivated by failure; only success promotes more success.*

Be Flexible. If your child seems frustrated by a certain activity because it's too difficult, stop! Do something else. Also, try not to drag an activity on forever. When your child begins to wiggle or lose interest, stop! Put the game away and don't coax or show disappointment. Learning should be fun. If you turn these activities into a chore, your child will become turned off and uncooperative. So relax and have fun. If s/he's not interested in working with you one day, don't take it as a personal insult.

Improvise, Explore and Invent new games yourself. The ideas in this handbook are only suggestions. If your child wants to change the rules of a game, great! S/he can be encouraged to think of variations for other games too. The materials required for these activities are inexpensive and simple to use. Most can be scrounged from neighborhood merchants or found among discarded junk. If you don't have a suggested item, think of other "litterbug materials" you might use as substitutes. You'll be surprised what imaginative and creative powers both you and your child have at inventing new and exciting ways to learn.

Good Luck and Have Fun!

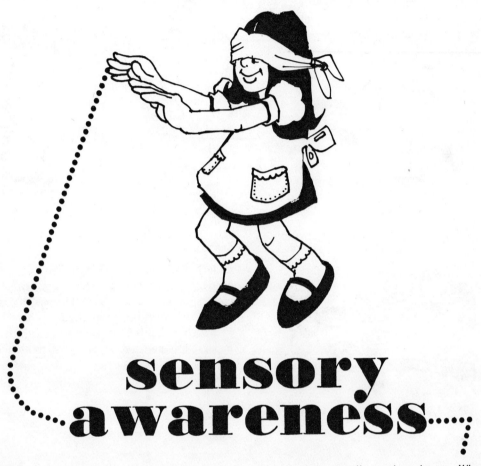

sensory awareness

Children learn about the world through their five senses—they see, hear, smell, touch and taste. When they are given the opportunity to manipulate and explore things in their own way, their awareness and understanding of the world is enriched. There is much you can do, however, to help your child become more sensitive to the experiences s/he encounters.

The activities in this section are designed to sharpen your child's senses. After doing some of these activities with your child, you should take every opportunity to encourage discussion about his or her experiences in terms of *all* the senses. For instance, if you have a picnic on the beach you can ask your child to describe how the air smells, how the salt water tastes, how the crashing waves sound, how the sand feels or how many seagulls s/he sees. Your child's vocabulary will expand and, more importantly, his or her appreciation of life will be enriched by an increased awareness of the sensory environment.

1

hearing

The Ticking Timer

Set a kitchen cooking timer for about five minutes then hide it somewhere in the house. Let your child hunt down the ticking sound before the bell goes off.

Listening Walk

Take a walk around your neighborhood and write down all the sounds you and your child hear. For example, you might hear the wind blowing, birds singing, an airplane passing overhead or a car horn.

Flip top bandage box

35 MM film can

Shake a Sound

Collect eight or ten 35 mm film cans or flip-top bandage boxes. Fill two of them with rice, two with thumbtacks, two with buttons and two with water. Mix them up. Your child will have fun trying to match the different sounds. You might also use paper clips, pebbles, popcorn or toothpicks to fill the cans.

Hear and Do

Give your child three simple commands such as "Walk to the table, turn around twice, and sit on the chair." After she has mastered a certain number of commands, make them more difficult and increase the number.

Finish It

Recite part of a nursery rhyme and have your child fill in a word, phrase or line using the rhyming words as a clue. For example:

Humpty Dumpty sat on a wall,
Humpty Dumpty had a great _____.

or

Hickory Dickory dock,
The mouse ran up the _____ .

Rhyming Riddles

Make up some riddles for a particular family of rhyming words and encourage your child to think of the answers by using rhyming clues. For example, here are some simple riddles for two different rhyming families (sat, hat, fat, bat, cat, rat and look, book, hook, crook, brook):

I'm thinking of a word that sounds like sat,
I wear it on my head, so it must be a _____ .

I'm thinking of a word that sounds like hat,
If I'm the opposite of skinny, I must be _____ .

I'm thinking of a word that sounds like fat,
When I play baseball, I must use a _____ .

I'm thinking of a word that sounds like bat,
It says meow, so it must be a _____ .

I'm thinking of a word that rhymes with look,
When I want to read, I open a _____ .

I'm thinking of a word that rhymes with book,
To hang up my coat I use a _____ .

I'm thinking of a word that rhymes with hook,
I use my eyes to see and _____ .

I'm thinking of a word that rhymes with look,
I use my pots and pans to _____ .

I'm thinking of a word that rhymes with cook,
Sometimes a thief is called a _____ .

I'm thinking of a word that rhymes with crook,
A small stream is called a _____ .

What Is It?

Ask your child to close his eyes. Make some familiar sounds and let him try to identify each one. For example, you might knock on the door, drop a pencil, clap your hands, snap your fingers, or bounce a ball.

Paper Cup Telephones

Punch a hole in the bottom of two paper cups or juice cans. Connect the two cups with a piece of string about 6 meters (20 feet) long. To keep the string from pulling through the holes, you might want to tie it to a piece of toothpick on the inside of the cup. Talk and listen to your child making sure the string is kept straight.

3

touching

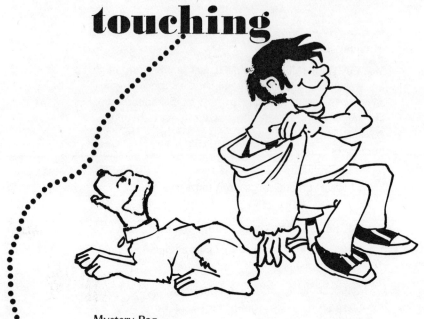

Mystery Bag

Collect several different objects and put them in an old pillow case. Your child will enjoy reaching into the bag, feeling an object and trying to guess what it is using only her sense of touch. Ask her questions about how each object feels. Is it soft? smooth? rough? hard? round? Does it have edges? Does it feel tickly? prickly? slippery? fuzzy? squishy? or fluffy? Some things you might want to include in the bag: a toothbrush, a rubber ball, a marble, a piece of sandpaper, a piece of rope, a small book or spoon.

How Does It Feel?

While your child is getting himself dressed in the morning, have him talk to you about how his different clothes feel. Are they soft? scratchy? stiff? limp? fuzzy? bumpy? or smooth?

Textured Rubbings

Place a piece of paper on top of different surfaces like tile, cement, frosted glass, or the radiator. Then rub on top of the paper with the flat side of a crayon.

Find It

Take a walk around your house and ask your child to find something that is hard, soft, rough or smooth. Something that is made of wood, plastic, metal, paper, glass, rubber, feathers or leather. Something that is hot, cold, sharp, dull, wet or dry.

Feel It On Your Toes

Your child might enjoy walking barefoot across different textured materials like a rug, a piece of paper, some wood, the sidewalk or some mud. Encourage her to describe how each different surface feels on her feet.

4

smelling

Sniff and Tell

Put into different baby jars: cloves, mint, flower petals, sawdust, ammonia, onions, cinnamon, cocoa, garlic, detergent, coffee, tobacco or anything else that has a strong odor. Blindfold your child. He will have fun trying to guess the contents of each jar by sniff alone. Encourage him to describe each of the odors . . . . does it remind him of a place he has visited or a particular food he has eaten?

Nose Walk

Walk around the neighborhood with your child and write down all the things you smell with your nose, such as gasoline fumes, flowers, a cake baking, freshly cut grass, garbage or pond water.

Smells I Like; Smells I Don't Like

Your child might want to look through a magazine and cut out pictures of things that are pleasant to smell and things that aren't. She can then paste these in a scrapbook that has been divided into two sections.

seeing

Observation Walk

Take a walk around the neighborhood with your child and play simple observation games. On one day you might see how many things he can find that are a particular color . . . a green car, a green bottle, a green roof, green grass. On another day he might try to find as many things as he can that have wheels and move . . . a wagon, a bicycle, a car or a bus.

What Did You See?

Hold up a detailed picture for a few moments and let your child study it. Put it away and ask her questions about the picture. "How many children were there in the picture?" "Was it daytime or night time?" Switch and let her ask you questions about a picture you look at.

I Spy

Look around the room, select an object and then describe it to your child. Give him one clue at a time until he guesses what it is. Then it is his turn to give clues to you.

Color Run

Call out a color and let your child run to touch something that is that color. Then let her call out a color for you to touch. Talk about the different shades of a color as you compare the things you touch.

What's Missing?

Put several objects on a table and let your child study them for a few minutes. Have him close his eyes while you remove one of the items. When he opens his eyes, have him guess what is missing. Now it's your turn.

tasting

Have a Tasting Party

Put several different foods on a plate and describe each as you and your child eat it. Is it sweet? salty? sour? tasteless? spicy? bitter? awful? or delicious? For example, try a saltine cracker, a piece of bread, lemon juice, salt water, sugar water, plain water, raisins, a pretzel, a marshmallow or a sour pickle.

Taster's Test

Blindfold your child and give her several different things to taste. See if she can figure out what they are by taste alone.

Tastes I Like; Tastes I Don't Like

Have your child make a scrapbook with two different sections. In the first section he can paste pictures from magazines of things he really likes to eat. In the second section he can paste pictures of things he'd rather not eat.

Yummy Toothpaste

Your child will enjoy making her own toothpaste by mixing 15 ml (1 tbsp.) baking soda, 5 ml (1 tsp.) salt and 5 ml (1 tsp.) of her favorite flavoring like vanilla, almond or peppermint. To keep fresh, store in a jar.

sensory awareness••

For the Child:

Do You Hear What I Hear? Helen Borton (Abelard-Schuman).

Handtalk, Remy Charlip (Parent's Magazine Press). A simple pictorial presentation of American Sign Language. Fascinating.

I Can't Said The Ant, Polly Cameron (Coward-McCann). Nonsense in rhyme.

Lisa and Her Soundless World, Edna Levine (Human Policy Press). A very touching story of a deaf child and how she copes.

Noisy Book, Margaret Wise Brown (Harper & Row). Yes, it's okay to be noisy sometimes, too!

The Sensible Book, Barbara Kay Polland (Celestial Arts). A celebration of the five senses.

The Very Hungry Caterpillar, Eric Carle (William Collins-World Publishing). Nibble, nibble, yum, yum ... simply delightful!

The Touch Me Book, Pat Witte (Western Publishing).

getting ready to read and write

There are many ways you as a parent can prepare your child for reading and writing. Beginning at an early age, read to your child as often as possible. A child will begin to love literature naturally if s/he is introduced to books in a friendly, non-threatening way. The more a child gets involved in books and the more curious s/he becomes about the written word, the greater the chances that s/he will want to learn to read and write.

Remember that story time should be fun for both of you. When you have read a story to your child, let him or her read it back to you. S/he may only be able to "read the pictures," but that's fine. Give a lot of help. Ask questions about the story and point out details in the pictures. Soon your child will begin to pick out familiar words and try to sound them out. Get a library card for your child and make frequent trips to the library. S/he can select interesting books and learn to care for them.

Your role as a model is also very important in the motivational aspects of reading. Parents who enjoy reading convey this attitude to their children. Keep in mind, too, that good language and vocabulary development are essential to good reading. Since good talkers usually make good readers, let your child know that what s/he says is important. If you listen —really listen—your child will gain confidence in his or her ability to communicate and be successful at self-expression.

9

letter recognition and letter sounds

Eat a Letter

Buy a package of alphabet cereal. Sprinkle a handful of letters on the table. Call out a letter and let your child scramble to find it. If she's right, she gets to eat the letter. After she becomes familiar with the letters, you might want to help her arrange them into names and words she knows. Alphabet soup noodles can also be used if you dip them into hot water, drain, and dry on waxed paper. That way they aren't quite as crunchy to eat.

Coil a Letter

Let your child roll play dough into long coils. (There is a good play dough recipe on page 40.) He can then practice forming these coils into the letters of his name. You might want to bake them to make the letters hard. Then he can mix up the letters and practice arranging them in the right order for his name. Or, make the letters out of cookie dough and let your child eat his name.

Sandpaper Letters

To help your child "feel" how the letters of the alphabet are made, cut out the different letters from dark sandpaper and mount on pieces of white shirt-backing cardboard. You can also do this with numbers and shapes.

Lines, Hooks and Humps

Talk about the different letters of the alphabet in terms of their distinguishing features so that your child will be able to identify them more easily. Letters are made up of lines, hooks and humps and are either open or closed. You might want to cut out an assortment of letter parts (long and short lines and big and little humps and hooks) and let your child practice fitting the pieces together to make the different letters of the alphabet.

Salty Letters

Pour some salt into a shallow pan and let your child practice making letters (or numbers) in the salt. You can color the salt by adding a little powdered tempera or colored chalk dust.

10

Sound Bags

For each letter sound that you and your child are working on, cut out a picture of something that begins with that sound and paste it onto a big paper bag. Your child can then put objects and pictures of things that begin with that sound into the bag. For example, if you are working on the sound for the letter B, you might want to cut out a picture of a bear to paste on the bag and collect things like a bell, bone, bib, box or ball to put in the bag.

Loony Letters

Make a large letter on a piece of paper with a crayon or a felt-tipped marker. Your child will have fun trying to make something unusual out of the letter.

Complete the Sentence

Let your child try to complete riddles by using a particular letter sound as a clue. For example, for the letter B:

> We sleep on a ———— .
> We learn many things by reading ———— .
> A fruit that is long and yellow is a ———— .
> When a child is very young he is called a ———— .

Silly Sentences

Make up several silly sentences and let your child try to pick out all the words in that sentence that begin with a particular letter sound. For example:

> B— *Billy* the *baker baked* a *bar* of soap in the *bottom* of the *birthday* cake. When we ate it we all *blew bubbles*.

Back Tracing

With your finger, trace a letter on your child's back. Have her try to guess what the letter is. Now it's her turn to draw a letter on your back and you try to guess what it is.

Letter Collage

Help your child search through a magazine for the letters that are in his name. Cut out the letters and paste them in order on a piece of paper. Underneath his name he might also want to paste words or pictures that are especially meaningful to him.

word power

Take a Trip

One of the surest ways to expand your child's vocabulary and improve her readiness for reading is to expose her to as many different learning situations as possible. Take her with you to the dry cleaners or shoe repair shop the next time you go. Even a simple errand can be turned into a valuable learning experience. Before you go, talk about what you will see. When you return, talk about what you saw and the people you met. Your child may want to draw a picture about her experience. Encourage her to tell you about the picture. If she wants you to, write a story at the bottom of the paper. Some places you might visit together . . . a park, zoo, museum, bakery, forest, railroad station, car wash, greenhouse, florist, kennel, lumber yard, airport, fish pond, construction site, fire station, police station or book store. Remember, a child's growth in language is directly related to the experiences she has had. Your role in providing those experiences is most important.

Words, Words, Everywhere

Take a walk with your child and write down all the words you see on signs, billboards and buses. He will probably be able to read many of them already like EXIT, DANGER, DO NOT TOUCH, ONE WAY, or KEEP OFF THE GRASS!

Part Of

Say a word or show a picture and let your child tell what it is a part of. For example, a wheel is part of a car, a buckle is part of a belt or a page is part of a book.

Position Words

Find a box large enough for your child to crawl into, then give her a number of instructions that involve understanding position. For example: "Stand *behind* the box." "Sit *inside* the box." "Put the paper *underneath* the box." Also use position words like next to, on top of, in the middle of or outside of.

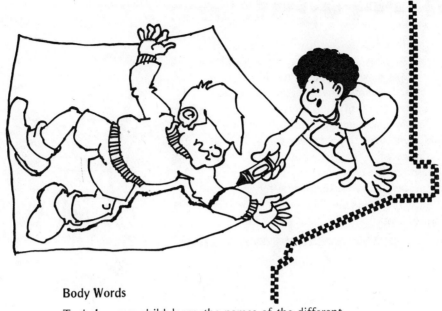

Body Words

To help your child learn the names of the different parts of the body, give him a series of easy instructions that involve body parts. For example, "Touch your nose." "Shake your leg." "Nod your head." Later you can throw in more difficult body parts and let him guess what they are . . . like ankle, thigh, shin, biceps, knuckles, palm, abdomen, cranium (head-bone), patella (kneecap) or clavicle (collar bone).

Body Puzzle

Have your child lay flat on the floor on a large piece of butcher paper. Trace around him. He can then color the body form and cut it into different parts. Then as he puts himself together, he can talk about each of the body parts and what its function is.

Opposites

There are many games you can make up that involve word opposites. When possible try to use real objects or pictures of things to help your child understand what is meant by opposite. Some opposites are:

wet-dry	long-short	walk-run	night-day
old-new	loud-quiet	good-bad	happy-sad
up-down	big-little	near-far	hard-soft
in-out	smile-frown	hot-cold	easy-hard

word recognition

When your child begins to identify and write down words, provide as many opportunities as you can for him to practice his new skills. Let him help you read simple recipes or the directions on packages. Encourage him to make lists of different things he does such as all the television programs he watches in one week, all the food he eats for three days or the household chores he is responsible for. Write notes and messages to your child often and encourage him to do the same. You might also ask him to take down telephone messages for you, write items on the grocery list or keep a "fix-it" list of household items that need repairing.

Tag It

Make a number of cards with different words printed on them . . . like table, chair, bed, desk or radio. Read the words and let your child attach the cards to the appropriate piece of furniture with masking tape. It won't be long before she'll be able to shuffle the cards and place them on the right objects all by herself.

How Do You Feel?

Help your child understand his moods and learn to read simple words at the same time. Make several cards with simple sentences printed on them . . . I feel happy, I feel sleepy, or I feel angry. Attach a piece of string to each end of the card so that your child can wear them around his neck. Let him suggest other words or phrases to print on cards.

Yes or No?

Make two cards, one with "yes" printed on it and the other with "no." Ask your child some questions and have her answer by flashing the appropriate card.

Newspaper Search

The newspaper is a great teaching tool for children. Let your child see how many words he can identify on a page. He will probably do quite well in the advertisement section and can read names of products he is familiar with.

writing stories and making books

Command Cards

Make a variety of cards with simple commands printed on them. Your child will have fun reading the cards and following the printed commands. At first the commands can be very easy, perhaps only one word like hop, sing, jump, smile or laugh. Later on you can make the words more difficult, such as walk to the door, look out the window, or clean up your room!

Making New Words

Give your child some examples of compound words . . . like sidewalk, butterfly, necktie, bedroom, cowboy, carport, or hairbrush. See if the two of you can dream up some more.

First, Middle, Last

To help your child understand that most people have a first, middle and last name, write her name using three separate cards. She can then practice putting her name in the proper order. Do the same with the names of other members of the family.

Binding Books

There are several ways to bind your child's books. You can simply staple the edges together or lace them together with yarn. Covers can be made from fabric scraps, wrapping paper, contact paper or wallpaper. If you want to preserve a particular book for a long time, you might want to make a cover out of cardboard or buy an inexpensive notebook binder.

Dictation

One way to increase your child's interest in words and speaking is to let him dictate stories to you. He will be delighted to see you write down his thoughts. Why not make a book out of some of his ideas. He can illustrate and you can write the story down for him on the opposite page. Don't worry about grammar or improper word usage. The most important thing is to give your child the confidence to express himself freely. When he begins to write words, he will want to write the captions for his illustrations himself.

Books, Books, Books

Encourage your child to make books on things that interest him (even if the subject doesn't appeal to you). You might suggest a *Touch Me Book* that has material of different textures pasted in it, an *Alphabet Book*, a *Shapes Book* or a *Poetry Book* with illustrations of his favorite poems. Also experiment making them different shapes and sizes.

classification and matching

Wallpaper Match

Mount a large piece of wallpaper on cardboard. Cut a duplicate piece of wallpaper into sections which will match the large section of wallpaper. Let your child practice matching the wallpaper pattern pieces by laying each piece on top of its corresponding pattern. The small pieces can be stored in a large envelope.

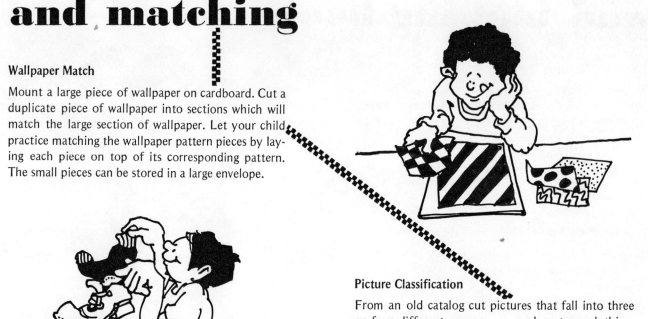

Things That Go Together

From an old catalog or magazine cut out pictures of things that usually go together . . . like shoes and socks, wallet and money, lamp and lampshade or cup and saucer. Scatter these pictures on the floor and let your child try to match the pictures of things that go together.

Picture Classification

From an old catalog cut pictures that fall into three or four different groups . . . such as toys, clothing, furniture, pets, fruits, vegetables or transportation. You can glue these pictures onto pieces of cardboard to make them last longer. Let your child practice sorting them into appropriate piles.

Touch and Match

Collect two each of a variety of items . . . 2 spoons, 2 jar lids, 2 pencils or 2 pieces of sand paper. Put one set of the items in a paper bag. Hand your child the others one at a time. Have him reach into the bag, feel around and try to find the match. No peeking!

Color Match

Cut a large circle out of cardboard. Divide it into eight sections and cover each with a different color of paper. Paint clothespins to match the colors on the circle. Your child can match the colors by clipping the clothespins to their corresponding colors.

Button Sort

Glue different styles of buttons to the bottom of each section of an egg carton. Place other matching buttons in a small container. Your child can sort these buttons by putting them into the appropriate sections of the egg carton.

skills that improve writing coordination

The most important thing that you can do to help your child build coordination for writing is to provide her with ample opportunity to use her muscles, both large and small. That means a lot of running, climbing, throwing, swinging, dancing, cutting, scribbling, painting and pasting. It is only after your child has developed these muscles that she will be able to coordinate her eye and hand movements to perform the difficult task of writing letters and numbers.

Tracing

Let your child trace a picture through very thin paper or trace around blocks and objects of various shapes and sizes.

Nuts and Bolts

Gather an assortment of nuts and bolts of different sizes. Mix them up in a container. Children delight in finding the corresponding sizes and screwing the nuts and bolts together. For very young children, use large nuts and bolts and limit the quantity.

Touch the Snake

Children often write their names from right to left when they first experiment with pencil and paper. To help your child improve his left to right orientation, place a squiggly snakelike line along the left-hand edge of a piece of paper. Have your child begin each line of writing by touching the snake and then "running away" by writing toward the right.

getting ready to read and write～～～～

For the adult:

Adams, Anne, *The Clock Struck One* (San Rafael, Ca.: Lewsing Press, 1973).

Ames, Louise Bates, *Stop School Failure* (New York: Harper and Row, 1972). Stresses the importance of the parent in identifying and correcting potential causes of school failure. Worthwhile reading *before* a child formally enters school.

Austin, John, *Ready Or Not?* (Muskegon, Mich.: Research Concepts, 1963). A checklist for school readiness.

Briggs, Dorothy, *Your Child's Self-Esteem* (New York: Doubleday, 1970). Self-esteem as an antecedent to success in reading.

Chall, J.S., *Learning To Read: The Great Debate* (New York: McGraw Hill, 1967). A critical evaluation of methods of instruction.

Hymes, J. L., *Before the Child Reads* (New York: Harper & Row, 1964).

Larrick, Nancy, *A Parent's Guide to Children's Reading* (New York: Bantam, 1975). Updated and revised edition of this classic reference for selecting reading material for children of all ages and every reading level.

Lee, D.M. and Allen, R.V., *Learning to Read Through Experience* (New York: Appleton-Century-Crofts, 1963). Using the child's own experiences as the starting point for building a relevant, meaningful reading vocabulary.

For the child:
Some tried-and-true favorites to enjoy over and over and over again.

All About Arthur, Eric Carle (Franklin-Watts).

Are You My Mother? P.D. Eastman (Random House).

The Boy Who Would Not Say His Name, Elizabeth Vreeken (Follett).

Brown Bear, Brown Bear, What Do You See? Bill Martin (Holt, Rinehart & Winston).

Curious George Learns The Alphabet, H.A. Rey (Houghton Mifflin).

A Fly Went By, Mike McClintock (Random House).

Harry the Dirty Dog, Gene Zion (Harper).

Laughing Camera for Children, Hanns Reich, edtor (Hill & Wang).

Make Way for Ducklings, Robert McCloskey (Viking).

Mr. Pine's Mixed-Up Signs, Leonard Kessler (Wonder Books).

Where the Wild Things Are, Maurice Sendak (Harper).

Whistle for Willy, Ezra Jack Keats (Viking).

William's Doll, Charlotte Zolotow (Harper & Row).

Will I Have a Friend? Miriam Cohen (Macmillan).

learning math concepts

There are endless opportunities to help your child when s/he is first learning math concepts. The activities you provide at home are essential for instilling the skills s/he will need throughout life. When you work with your child, however, keep in mind that s/he will understand math concepts better if s/he works directly with concrete objects. In other words, if your child is learning to count, make sure that all the objects s/he is counting are physically present. Whether s/he is counting the napkins on the dinner table, the pillows on the sofa or the buttons on a shirt, have your child touch each object as s/he says the appropriate number. Also remember that children build on what they already know; so use every opportunity possible to review what s/he has learned previously. S/he will be far more willing to try a hand at more difficult tasks is s/he has been successful many times with activities s/he has already mastered.

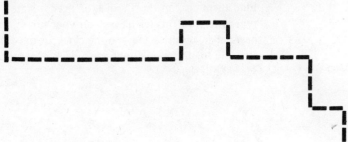

using numbers and counting things

Footprints

Trace around your child's foot on ten pieces of cardboard. Cut out the footprints. Number them from 1-10. Have him arrange them in order and practice counting while he walks, or mix them up and call out different numbers for him to jump on.

Number Cards

With a felt-tipped marker or black crayon, make large numbers (0-10) on pieces of cardboard that are approximately 15 cm x 22 cm (6'' x 9''). Your child can practice arranging her number cards in the proper sequence. Keep in mind, however, that understanding number concepts means far more than being able to count to a high number or arrange numbers in their proper order. To help your child understand that numbers are associated with different quantities, you might want to give her a box full of objects (1 pinecone, 2 buttons, 3 clothespins, 4 spoons, 5 paperclips . . . and so on) and let her arrange the objects next to the appropriate card.

Numbers, Numbers Everywhere

Find them . . . on the TV dial, on license plates, on a typewriter, on the telephone, on your house, in the newspaper, on price tags, on the clock, at the grocery store, in the telephone book, on a deck of cards or on speed limit signs.

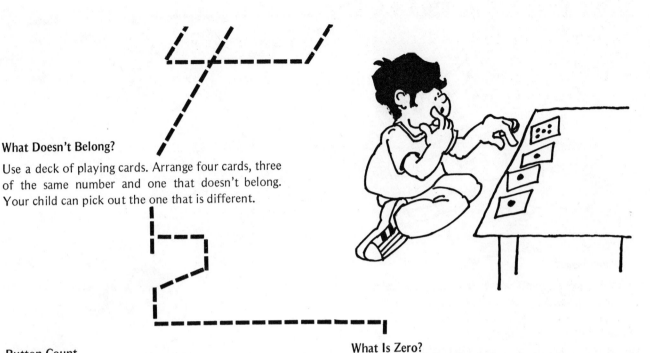

What Doesn't Belong?

Use a deck of playing cards. Arrange four cards, three of the same number and one that doesn't belong. Your child can pick out the one that is different.

Button Count

Number the compartments of a muffin tin from 0-11. Provide your child with 66 buttons. Let him place the correct number of buttons in each compartment. If he is correct, all the buttons will be used up.

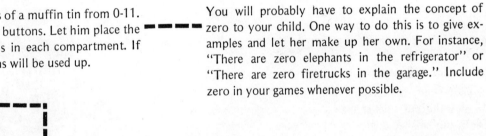

What Is Zero?

You will probably have to explain the concept of zero to your child. One way to do this is to give examples and let her make up her own. For instance, "There are zero elephants in the refrigerator" or "There are zero firetrucks in the garage." Include zero in your games whenever possible.

Take a Survey

Take a survey of your home. Count and write down how many chairs, windows, pillows, pictures and toothbrushes you have. Let your child think of other things to count and record.

size

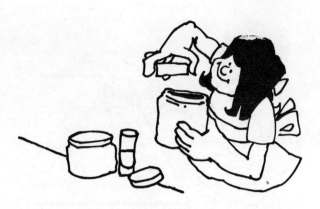

Scrambled Lids

Make a collection of many different sized jars. Save the lids. Put them all in a box and let your child figure out which lid fits which jar.

Large and Small

On a table place several pairs of different objects that are the same except for size. For example, a large plate and a small one, a large sponge and a small sponge, a large spoon and a small one, or use glasses, balls, scissors, records or books. Have your child sort them according to size, putting all the large objects on one half of the table and all the smaller ones on the other half of the table.

What Is Large?

Ask your child to find something that is . . . larger than a peanut but smaller than a pear . . . larger than a pencil but smaller than a telephone pole . . . larger than a cat but smaller than a kangaroo. Think of others.

ordering

The Line Up

Collect four to six bottles of the same type (syrup or soda bottles are good). Fill up the bottles with different amounts of colored water, leaving one bottle completely empty. Seal all the bottles. Your child can practice putting the bottles in order from the least to the most.

Short to Long

Cut up several drinking straws so they are different lengths. Have your child arrange them in order from shortest to longest. Begin with only three straw lengths and gradually increase the number as your child masters each level of difficulty. You might also want to use cardboard tubes like those used for paper towels or toilet paper; however, these are more difficult to cut.

shape

Shape a Rope

Make large shapes on the floor with an old rope or clothesline. You might want to give your child directions to follow using whatever shape he has just made . . . jump in and out of the circle . . . put one leg in the triangle and the other leg out . . . sit in the square.

Circle Puzzle

Cut several large circles from cardboard or heavy paper. Then cut the circle into two or three parts making an interesting pattern along the cut edge. Let your child practice putting the pieces together.

Find It

Look inside or outside your house for different shapes.

Round:	buttons, spools, clocks, bottlecaps, coins, dishes, doorknobs, jars, wheels, records.
Square:	matchbooks, bolts, dice, windowpanes, postage stamps, sugar cubes.
Triangle:	TV antenna, earrings, a sailboat sail, "Yield" signs, rooftops.
Rectangle:	doors, tables, books, piano seats, baking pans, a bathroom mirror, cereal boxes.

Make a Shape

Cut an assortment of traingles from cardboard or heavy paper. Vary the sizes of the triangles so that when fit together they will make a larger triangle or another geometric shape. Let your child have fun arranging them into interesting patterns and shapes. More durable shapes can be cut from balsa wood or from very thin plywood.

Stretch-It Board

Pound ten to fifteen nails in a random pattern half way into a board that is approximately 23 cm x 30 cm (9" x 12"). Let your child practice making interesting shapes by stretching colored rubber bands around the nails.

measuring, weighing and balancing things

Weigh and Record

Using the bathroom scale, weigh and record how many kilograms your child weighs. Then let her think of other things to weigh . . . like you.

Make a Scale

Cut off the bottom section of a hanger. Attach three strings to each end. These strings can be stapled or tied to two balancing dishes made from pie tins or plastic coffee can lids. Hang the hooked section of the hanger on a door knob or railing so that it can swing freely. Weigh and balance different things: three pencils and two pinecones, four acorns and one clothespin. Let your child think of other things to balance and weigh.

Balancing Blocks

Lay a board that is about 60 cm (2 feet) long and 10 cm (4") wide on top of a fulcrum 8 cm (3" dowel cut in half). Mark the board into different units and let your child practice balancing smaller blocks on it.

How Long?

Let your child experiment measuring things with a meter stick. It doesn't matter how accurate he is at first. What is important is that he is beginning to use comparison words like longer, shorter, wider and narrower.

Help your child think of imaginative ways to measure different things around the house. For example, "the book is five hands long," "the dog is ten pencils long," "the foot is twenty pennies long."

After repeated experiences in measuring in this informal way, your child will begin to see the need for standard units of measurement. Only then will words like centimeter, decimeter and meter have any relevance.

time

How Long Does It Take?

Using a timer or the minute hand on a clock, let your child see how long it takes him to get dressed, brush his teeth or watch a program on television.

What Is a Minute?

Let your child guess how many times she can touch her toes in one minute, how many cars will pass the house in one minute or how many crackers she can eat in one minute. Then check. Let her think of other guessing games that will instill the concept of one minute.

Paper Plate Clock

Help your child make the numbers from 1-12 around the edge of a paper plate so that the plate resembles a clock. With a brad, attach two hands in the center of the clock. Set the clock to show your child what time Sesame Street comes on, what time dinner will be ready or what time he goes to bed. To help him become familiar with "time" words, use them often. For instance: "We will eat in fifteen minutes," "The show begins at two o'clock," or "The cookies will take one half an hour to bake."

learning math concepts ------------

For the adult:

Burns, Marilyn, *I Hate Mathematics! Book* (Boston: Little & Brown, 1975). Imaginative, fun ways to instill important mathematical concepts in children. Geared primarily for elementary-age children but can be simplified for preschoolers also.

Copeland, Richard, *How Children Learn Mathematics* (New York: Macmillan, 1974). Implications of Piaget's theory to instruction of mathematical concepts in early childhood education as well as the elementary and junior high school levels.

Hirsch, Elisabeth, *The Block Book* (Washington, D.C.: National Association for the Education of Young Children, 1974). The importance of block play for instilling important math concepts.

Piaget, Jean, *The Psychology of the Child* (New York: Basic Books, 1969). Definitive presentation of the development of logico-mathematical concepts in young children.

Sharp, Evelyn, *Thinking Is Child's Play* (New York: Avon, 1969). Homemade games and activities for math.

U.S. Department of Commerce, *What About Metric?* (Washington, D.C.: Superintendent of Documents, #030-01191). Simple introduction to thinking metric.

For the child:

Biggest House In The World, Leo Lionni (Pantheon).

Brian Wildsmith's 1, 2, 3's, Brian Wildsmith (Franklin Watts).

Counting Carnival, Flenie Ziner (Coward-McCann).

500 Hats of Bartholomew Cubbins, Dr. Seuss (Vanguard).

A Giraffe and a Half, Shel Silverstein (Harper & Row).

One & One & One, Louis Untermeyer (Crowell & Collier).

Over in the Meadow, John Langstaff (Harcourt, Brace & Co.).

Seasame Street Book of Numbers, Children's Television Workshop (Preschool Press, Time-Life).

Ten Apples Up On Top, Theo LeSieg (Random House, Beginner Books).

discovery
through science

The inquisitive nature of children makes them natural scientists. They continually search to find out the how, why, what and where of things around them. Encourage this kind of questioning and exploring. Give your child as many opportunities as possible to investigate, examine and experiment. By piecing together bits and pieces of information, s/he will gradually begin to understand some of the puzzling and intriguing aspects of the world in which s/he lives.

plants and seeds

Watch It Sprout

Stick two or three toothpicks into the top portion of a carrot. Lay the toothpicks on the rim of a small glass or container of water so that the bottom of the carrot is in the water. Watch it sprout and grow in a few days. Also try growing beets, radishes, onions and turnips in the same way.

Seeds and Pits

Let your child make a collection of different kinds of seeds and pits like those from an orange, a watermelon, grapes, a sunflower or a peach. He might also enjoy growing some seeds and pits like those from a pumpkin, apple, dates, prunes or an avocado. Place the seeds in water in a sunny spot and be very patient. Eventually they will split and begin to sprout. At that point you can either plant them in soil or leave them in water.

Sweet Potato Plant

Stick three or four toothpicks around the middle of a sweet potato or yam. Place it in a container of water so the toothpicks support the potato on the rim of the container. Place in some sunlight and replenish water when it gets to a low level. In several weeks it will sprout into a beautiful plant.

That Fuzzy Stuff Called Mold

Leave a piece of bread out overnight. The following day place it in a closed jar and put the jar in a damp warm place. Watch the mold grow in a few days. Mold is also fascinating to look at with a magnifying glass.

Sponge Grass

Put a sponge in a small saucer of water to keep it moist. Sprinkle some grass seed on top of the sponge . . . and in a few days . . . Presto!

The Long Journey

To help your child understand how plants get their food, explain that inside a plant there are many roads that the food travels on to get to the top of the plant. These roads are called veins. The food from the ground (water and minerals) travels up the plant's roots into the veins and feeds the plant. You might want to get a large leaf and point out the veins on the leaf. You might also want to do the following experiment. Put a celery stalk into a glass of colored water. Watch the leaves turn the color of the water in a few hours. Cut across the stalk and point out the veins to your child.

air

What Is It?

Explain to your child that we can't see air or taste it but we still know that it's there. To help her understand, take her outside to watch a tree, a kite or a flag blow in the wind. Use an air pump to inflate a bicycle tire or let her blow up a balloon. You might also want to try the following experiment. Place a napkin in the bottom of a glass. Place the glass upside down into a bowl of water. Let your child see how the glass does not fill up with water and the napkin stays dry. Now tilt the glass so that bubbles rise to the surface of the water. What happens?

What Is a Bubble? Make Some.

Mix together in a baby jar 60 ml (¼ cup) liquid dish detergent, 120 ml (½ cup) water, and a few drops of food coloring. You might also add 5 ml (1 tsp.) of glycerine to make the bubbles longlasting. Glycerine can be purchased at most hardware stores. Provide your child with a plastic straw or twist a wire to make a bubble blower. Great fun!

water

Sink Or Float?

Collect a variety of different objects like a cork, penny, bottle cap, pencil, paperclip, ping pong ball, rubber band or a piece of soap. Let your child guess whether each of these things will sink or float. Give her a bowl of water and let her test whether or not her guess was correct. She might also enjoy making a walnut boat to float. Put a small piece of play dough into the hollow of a walnut half. Put a toothpick through a triangular piece of paper and secure it in the play dough. Then float it. Make a whole fleet of walnut boats and sail them in the bath tub.

Water Is Water, Or Is It?

The next time it rains, let your child put a bowl outside to catch some rain water. Fill up another bowl with regular faucet water. Get two handkerchiefs and dip one into the rain water and the other into a bowl of faucet water. Let them dry. Compare how the handkerchiefs feel. Then let your child stir a capful of dishsoap into each bowl and compare how the two types of water make suds.

Making Rainbows

Adjust a hose to make a fine spray. Stand with your back to the sun and watch the rainbow of colors in the water spray.

Evaporation

Place a jar of water in the sun. Mark the water level on the side of the jar with a black crayon or felt-tipped marker. Observe what happens to the water after a few hours, a day or two days.

Making Rain

Fill a small pan with ice and hold it over a boiling kettle. Let your child observe when the hot steam hits the bottom of the small pan.

temperature

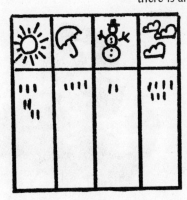

Melting Away

Let your child record the time it takes for an ice cube to melt in the refrigerator, on the radiator or outside on a sunny day.

Seasons Scrapbook

Let your child make a scrapbook for the different seasons. Under the appropriate headings, Spring, Summer, Fall and Winter, he can paste pictures of suitable clothing, activities or nature scenes.

Weather Tally

Help your child make a chart to record the weather in your city for one month. Each day she can mark the chart according to the weather outside. Then add up all the marks at the end of the month. She might want to do it again during another season to see if there is any difference in the weather.

light

Spot It

Let your child place a small mirror in a glass of water. Adjust the glass until the sun shines on the mirror. The mirror should reflect a rainbow of colors against the wall or ceiling. He might also want to hold the mirror in his hands while standing in the sun and make the spot of light bounce around the room. Spot it and catch it.

Leaf Prints

Collect an assortment of interesting leaves. Place them on a piece of colored paper out in the sun for a few hours. Remove the leaves and see what the sunlight has created on the paper.

The Broken Pencil

Put a pencil in a glass of water. Let your child look at it from the side of the glass. The refraction of light will cause it to look broken.

Shadow Play

Hang a sheet across a doorway. Put a light behind the sheet and let your child have fun creating different shadows while he stands between the light and the sheet. If you sit in front of the sheet you can watch the performance. Shadows are also fun to watch (and try to catch) outside. Take your child outside at different times on a sunny day to compare the length of the shadows his body makes.

magnets and magnifying glasses

Magnifying Magic

Next time your child's birthday comes around, buy him a magnifying glass. You'll be amazed at the hours of entertainment he'll derive from this educational toy. Let him examine a piece of skin, a penny, some pond water, a nylon stocking or an insect. Here are a few experiments that are especially exciting to observe with a magnifying glass.

- Put about 45 ml (3 tbsps.) of baking soda in a small jar. Add a small amount of vinegar. Stir and watch what happens.

- Put an egg white in a small jar of water. Observe the change over a few days.

Make It Move

Float several metal bottle caps in a bowl of water. By holding a magnet near the caps (but not touching them) your child can move the bottle caps wherever she directs them. She can also scatter thumb tacks on a piece of cardboard. While you support the cardboard, she can move the magnet underneath to make the thumb tacks move on top.

Pick Up

Collect a variety of different objects like a rubber band, paper clip, penny, hairpin, safety pin, thumbtack, straight pin or a jar lid. Ask your child to guess which objects the magnet will pick up; then she can experiment with the magnet to see if her guesses were correct.

Machine Hunt

Take a walk around your house with your child and look for as many different kinds of machines as you can find . . . like a pencil sharpener, egg beater, can opener, record player, typewriter, clock or a vacuum cleaner. Also look for simple machines like a pair of scissors or a hole puncher.

Pinch Up

Provide your child with a pair of tongs, a clothespin and some tweezers. Have him practice picking things up with them to help him understand what these simple machines have in common.

Don't Throw It Away

The next time an old clock, egg timer or wrist watch breaks, don't throw it away. Give it to your child and let her take it apart and play with it.

discovery through science ~~~~~~

For the adult:

Cobb, Vicki, *Science Experiments You Can Eat* (New York: Lippincott, 1972). The activities in this handbook are geared primarily for older children, but with a little extra guidance and help are also fun and exciting for preschoolers

Chevron Chemical Company, *A Child's Garden*. Available free by writing to Chevron Chemical Company, 200 Bush Street. San Francisco 94120. Contains numerous plant projects to do with young children

Euston, Carol *A Better Place to Be· A Guide to Environmental Learning* (Washington. D.C.: Superintendent of Documents # 2400-00805). Good guide for instilling environmental awareness in young children

Fiarotta, Phyllis, *Snips & Snails and Walnut Whales* (New York: Workman Publishing Co., 1975). Nature crafts by the dozens.

Frankel, Lillian and Godfrey, *101 Best Nature Games and Projects* (New York: Gramercy Publishing Co. 1959).

McGavack, John, *Guppies, Bubbles and Vibrating Objects* (New York: John Day, 1969). Variety of projects that instill important science concepts.

Petrich, Patricia, *The Kid's Garden Book* (Concord, Ca.: Nitty Gritty, 1974). Guaranteed to turn your thumb green.

Russell, Helen Ross, *Ten Minute Fieldtrips* (Chicago: J.G. Ferguson, 1973). An indispensable resource guide for anyone interested in environmental education.

Vivian, Charles, *Science Experiments & Amusements for Children* (New York: Dover Publications, 1963). Many good projects.

For the child:

All Around You, Jeanne Bendick (McGraw).

Animal Friends, Judy Dunn (Creative Education).

The Carrot Seed, Ruth Krauss (Scholastic Books).

Mickey's Magnet, Franklin M. Branley (Crowell).

The Storm Book, Charlotte Zolotow (Harper).

You Will Go to the Moon, Mae and Ira Freeman (Random House).

The following publishers also publish excellent science books:

Franklin Watts—*Let's Find Out Science Books*
National Geographic—*Books for Young Explorers*
Children's Press—*True Book Series*
Grossett & Dunlap—*Living Science Books*

Two excellent science publications for young children are:

Ranger Rick's Nature Magazine	*World Magazine*
Available from The National Wildlife Federation 1412 16th Street NW Washington, D.C. 20036	Available from National Geographic Society 17th & M Streets Washington, D.C. 20036
$6/year (10 issues)	$4.85/year (12 issues)

creating through art and music

Art and music are non-verbal ways your child communicates ideas and feelings about the world. Since creative endeavors are personal expressions, they reflect a child's unique individuality. In this type of communication, it is the *process* of creating that should be stressed and not the final product. In other words, the sensations and enjoyment your child experiences when s/he fingerpaints are far more important than the final picture. Similarly, what is important in music is the way a child feels and responds inside when s/he hears musical rhythms.

The activities in this section are designed to help stretch your child's imagination and express his or her individuality. When doing an art project, try to give your child as few instructions as possible. Avoid comparing and judging. Don't show your child how to draw an object. S/he'll merely want to copy what you have done and this defeats the whole purpose of the activity. A child's competence in artistic creativity will unfold naturally if s/he is allowed to develop at his or her own rate. So be patient and provide ample opportunities to explore new modes of expression. Encourage creative endeavors by displaying your child's art work around the house and talking about what s/he has done.

painting

Easel Paint Recipe

To get the most for your money, buy dry tempera powder. Each time you need paint, you can mix a small amount of the powder with water. The paint consistency should be like thick cream. Adding a  little detergent will make the paint wash out more easily. You might also try adding a small amount of liquid starch or baby oil to the mixed paint for an interesting effect. Start your child with the primary colors first (red, blue and yellow). Later he can practice mixing these colors in different combinations to produce green, orange and purple. He can paint on old paper bags, butcher paper, old gift wrapping paper or plain newsprint (from your newspaper).

Improvise

Your child can produce imaginative works of art *without* paint brushes. She can dip a string into a container of paint and swirl it on a piece of paper or make a creepy spider picture by blowing a blotch of paint around on a piece of paper with an ordinary drinking straw. She can also produce interesting pictures with Q-tips, an old toothbrush, an eye dropper, an old bottle brush or a roll-on deodorant bottle that has been filled with paint.

Footprints and Handprints

Do this project outside on a sunny day. Let your child paint his hands and feet with easel paint, then quickly print on a piece of large paper. You might also place the paint in a shallow pan so he can step into it and then hop around on the paper.

Shine-Through Painting

Spread some salad oil over a picture your child has just painted. When you hang it in a window, the light will shine through.

Soap Snow

Whip about 480 ml (2 cups) soap flakes with 120 ml (½ cup) of water to the consistency of whipped cream. Put on paper to use as fingerpaint or in a pastry tube to be squeezed out into a design.

Drip and Squish

Let your child drip some paint on one half of a piece of paper. Fold over the other half and press. Open up.

Crayon Painting

Melt crayon scraps in a muffin pan over boiling water. Using a brush, your child can paint designs onto an old sheet, apron, cloth napkin, shirt or smock. Iron the material and the colors will stay in permanently.

Printing

Cut an orange, lemon, potato, carrot or pear into a variety of interesting shapes. Let your child dip these items into a shallow dish of paint and then press them on a piece of paper. You can suggest that she make the printing object "hop like a bunny" across the piece of paper so the paint won't smear. Let her experiment printing with other gadgets around the house . . . like hair curlers, sponges, nuts and bolts, kitchen utensils, bottle caps, clothespins, cookie cutters, or crumpled paper. Be prepared for a mess.

crayons, scissors, paper and paste

Paste Recipe

Mix 240 ml (1 cup) flour with 240 ml cold water. Add to 800 ml (3¼ cups) boiling water. Cook until the mixture is clear. Add 5 ml (1 tsp.) alum as a preservative. Store in tightly covered jars.

Glue Tip

Some of the art projects in this section call for glue instead of paste. You will save money in the long run if you buy a large container of Elmers at a discount hardware store. Then stretch your investment by mixing 15 ml (1 tbsp.) glue with 30 ml (2 tbsp.) water each time your child needs some glue.

Paper Is Paper, Or Is It?

Don't limit your child's artistic endeavors to plain white paper. Let him experiment coloring on as many different kinds as possible . . . like sandpaper, butcher paper, paper towels, graph paper, paper napkins, the want ads section from a newspaper, wallpaper scraps, toilet paper, cardboard, paper bags, freezer paper (try both sides), adding machine paper, discarded computer print-out paper or paper cut into different shapes. If you have any carbon paper around, give your child a piece or two to experiment with. He'll think it's magic to see his artistic creations come out in duplicate or triplicate.

Also, raid the trash basket at your local picture framing store. These art stores often discard pieces of matting that are ideal for art projects.

Peel Off

Peel off the paper around a few of your child's crayons. Put notches or grooves in them and let your child color by rubbing the crayons on their side onto a piece of paper.

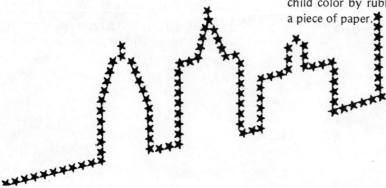

Eraser Picture

Cover a piece of paper with pencil marks using the side of the lead. Your child can then "draw" a picture by erasing away the lead into whatever design he wants.

Color Press

Using an ordinary kitchen grater, help your child grate old crayons into many small shavings. Arrange these shavings on a piece of waxed paper. Cover with another piece of waxed paper the same size. Press with a hot iron . . . Wow!

Box People

Collect several cardboard boxes of different shapes and sizes. Help your child construct box people by taping the boxes together and paint on appropriate features. Yarn, steel wool or Easter grass can be glued on for hair. She might also want to glue on empty spools for the eyes and a bottle cap for the nose.

Crayon Resist

Your child can make a crayon resist by pressing very hard with the crayons while she makes a design on a piece of heavy paper. Then paint over the entire picture with thin black or purple paint and watch the crayon design show through.

Patchwork Picture

Cut out an assortment of different material scraps. Let your child patch a picture together by glueing the material scraps onto a piece of heavy paper or cardboard.

Paper Towel Design

Fold a piece of paper towel several times. Dip the corners of the towel into different colors of food coloring mixed in water. Unfold the towel and spread out to dry.

modeling, mobiles and other things

Play Dough Recipe

Mix together 800 ml (3¼ cups) flour and 240 ml (1 cup) salt. Add 360 ml (1½ cups) water, several drops of food coloring and 15 ml (1 tbsp.) salad oil.

Cornstarch Recipe for Modeling Dough

Mix together 240 ml (1 cup) cornstarch and 360 ml (1½ cups) baking soda. Add 240 ml cold water and several drops of food coloring.

Twig Mobile

Attach a piece of string to an unusually shaped twig. Suspend it from the ceiling or a doorway entrance. From this twig your child can hang any number of different objects . . . like pictures cut from magazines and glued to different shapes of cardboard, play dough objects that have been baked and painted, or different letters, numbers and shapes that have been cut from colored paper and attached to strings.

Bake It and Save It

Either one of the above recipes can be baked after your child has created something she wants to keep forever. Bake the play dough recipe for about 45 minutes at 150° C. (300° F.). Bake the cornstarch recipe for 1½ hours at 120° C. (250° F.). The objects can then be painted with easel paint. Why not hang some of your child's creations on the Christmas tree as ornaments?

Straw Mobile

Let your child cut out interesting shapes from paper. Then with a needle and thread he can alternate stringing different lengths of paper straws and his cut out shapes. Tie a knot after the last shape. These chains can be attached to a hanger. Suspend the hanger from a doorway entrance.

Flying Disc

Cut circles of varying sizes out of stiff paper or cardboard; then cut a narrow pie slice out of the circle. Your child will enjoy tossing them through the air (preferably outside).

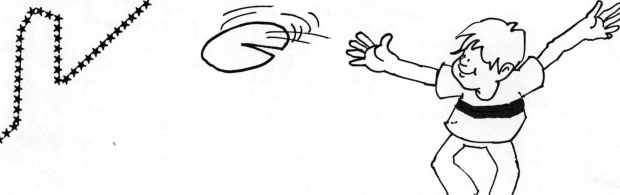

Fingerprint Stationery

Let your child experiment with an old stamp pad making interesting finger and thumb prints. Add a few wings, feet or a face and you've got fingerprint creatures. You might want to put these prints on the upper left hand corner of blank white paper and use the paper as stationery. These fingerprint creatures could also be made on the back flap of the envelopes for the stationery.

Sewing Cards

Punch holes in cardboard pieces which have been cut in various shapes and sizes. Your child can practice lacing in and out the holes with a long colorful shoelace or a piece of yarn (stiffen the ends of the yarn by wrapping tape around them). When he has mastered the ins and outs of this activity, you might want to number the holes so he can follow a particular pattern.

Jigsaw Puzzle

Let your child pick out an interesting picture from an old magazine. Glue this picture onto a piece of cardboard which has been cut the same size. Shellac and cut into a number of interesting pieces to form a puzzle. Your child might also want to make a puzzle out of one of his favorite drawings.

Twirlies

Dip a piece of yarn into a dish of liquid starch. Arrange the yarn in an interesting shape or pattern on a piece of waxed paper. Put another piece of waxed paper on top and flatten between some books. The yarn should be dry and stiff in about 24 hours. Attach a string and suspend in a doorway entrance.

litterbug art

Collages

Interesting collages can be made from many things you would ordinarily throw away. Simply provide your child with a variety of litterbug materials and some paste or glue; her imagination will carry on from there. Things to save: bottle caps, steel wool pads, toothpicks, string, rubber bands, old ribbons, burned out flash bulbs, popsicle sticks, used gift wrapping paper, old sponges, sawdust, jar lids, bark, nut shells, cupcake or candy papers, material scraps, pebbles, acorns, nuts, bolts, washers, old jewelry, tinsel, buttons, magazine pictures, comics from the Sunday newspaper, old buckles, shoelaces, broken zippers, styrofoam packing, Easter grass, straws, tile or scraps of linoleum, rug scraps, old golf tees, pebbles or feathers.

Newspaper Animals

Don't throw away those old newspapers; save them to make a whole collection of stuffed animals. Put four large pieces on top of one another. With a crayon, draw the shape of an animal such as a turtle or a fish on the top piece. Keeping all four pieces together, have your child cut out the animal shape. Staple along the edges except for a small opening. Stuff with wads of newspaper. Each side of the animal should be two pieces thick. Staple closed and paint.

Making Blocks

Instead of throwing away used milk cartons, make blocks out of them for your child. Wash out the insides of two cartons and cut off the top sections. Then fit one carton inside the other. Tape closed. Let your child paint them different colors and designs. If you add a small amount of detergent to the paint it will adhere to the waxy surface of the cartons. Another way to make blocks is to cut old lumber scraps into different shapes and sizes and sand until smooth.

sculpturing

Soap Sculptures

Leave a bar of Ivory Soap unwrapped for 24 hours. Give your child a small dull kitchen knife and let him chip away at the soap.

Wire Sculptures

The next time the telephone man installs a telephone in your neighborhood, ask him for extra pieces of colored telephone wire. They're great fun to twist and turn and make sculptures out of.

Ice Sculptures

Wash out a large milk carton and fill with water. Freeze. Peel off the carton. Provide your child with a screw driver and a small hammer and let her chisel away. A good activity to be done in the shade on a hot summer day.

Styrofoam Sculptures

The next time you buy something that is packed in styrofoam, save the styrofoam pieces and cut them into interesting shapes. Your child can make an unusual sculpture by sticking toothpicks, popsicle sticks, wire, hairpins, pencils and paperclips into the styrofoam pieces.

Wood Sculptures

Collect an assortment of wood scraps that are different sizes and shapes from your local lumber yard. Your child can glue these pieces together to form an interesting sculpture. He might want to add on cardboard tubes, empty spools, popsicle sticks or pieces of corrugated cardboard.

fun with food

Finger-Licking Fun

Let your child help you mix a box of cake mix according to the directions but omit the eggs. Separate the mix into two or three bowls and make each a different color with food coloring. Fill a pastry tube and let your child squeeze out a design on a piece of cardboard. If you don't have a pastry tube, the cake mix can be squeezed out of an empty detergent bottle or simply dripped from a spoon above the paper. Let these creations dry for a full day or two. You shouldn't have any problem getting your child to help you clean up after this project!

Gumdrop Giraffe

Use a large gumdrop for the body of the giraffe. Legs, neck and tail are made by poking a hairpin through raisins. Add a small gumdrop for the head and brightly colored paper for the eyes, ears and mouth. Now think of other crazy creatures to make.

Beads

Color elbow or shell macaroni by dipping it into a dish of water and food coloring then drying it on a piece of waxed paper. Your child will enjoy stringing these noodles to make an assortment of necklaces, love beads or bracelets to wear. Necklaces, beads and bracelets can also be made out of empty thread spools, play dough balls or cut-up drinking straws.

Bean Mosaic

Provide your child with an assortment of different dried beans like kidney, pinto or lima. When glued to a piece of cardboard, they make an interesting mosaic.

Rice Designs

Your child will enjoy dripping glue onto a colored piece of paper into an interesting design. She can then sprinkle rice over the entire paper. Let dry and shake off the excess. Salt, sand or sawdust may also be used.

Popcorn Pictures

Let your child help you make up a batch of popcorn. He can then glue the popcorn (and some unpopped kernels) on a piece of heavy paper or cardboard to make an unusual kind of picture.

Yummy Fingerpaint

Mix a box of chocolate pudding. Spread onto a cookie sheet and let your child have fun fingerpainting designs. She probably won't want to stop this activity until she's eaten up all her fingerpaint.

Scented Ball

Poke cloves into an apple or orange until it is completely covered. Let it stand near a radiator or in the sunlight for three or four days. Tie a ribbon into a bow and attach to the top of the scented ball. This will make a nice gift for a relative or friend to hang in their closet.

Spaghetti Swirl

Cook spaghetti until just limp. It should be fairly sticky. Let your child arrange the strands of spaghetti one at a time on a piece of heavy paper. The spaghetti will stick by itself.

Eggshell Vases

Save those eggshells from your morning breakfast. Dip into food coloring and let dry. Crunch into tiny pieces. Spread glue over the outside of a Coca-Cola or dark beer bottle. Sprinkle the crushed eggshells on top of the glue. This makes a beautiful vase to give as a gift.

45

puppets

Egg Head Puppet

Poke a small hole into one end of an uncooked egg. Drain out the contents. Enlarge the hole to fit on your child's finger. Add facial features with colored felt-tipped markers. Glue on pieces of yarn for hair.

Fly Swatter Puppet

Glue wire, foil, cotton or paper features to the flat side of a fly swatter. Manipulate by holding the handle.

Snake

Use an old colorful knee sock. Tuck in the tip of the toe for the snake's mouth and add a piece of red felt for his tongue. Glue or sew on buttons for his eyes.

Felt Puppet

Cut out two identical pieces of felt in the shape indicated. Make sure they are big enough for your child's hand to fit inside. Sew the sides together and glue on features cut from felt scraps.

Flying Ghost

Tie a square piece of sheet or an old handkerchief over a ball of cotton. Features can be added with a black felt-tipped marker. Add a stick inside to make the ghost move or fly him through the air by attaching a piece of string.

Cereal Box Cat

Use a small cereal box. Cut in half on three sides. Fold back leaving two openings to slip thumb and fingers into. Uncut side becomes the mouth. Paint and glue on ears, eyes, nose, tongue and whiskers.

Spoon Puppet

Cut a strip of material that is about 8 cm x 16 cm (3" x 6"). Gather it around the neck of a serving spoon. Secure with a wire or string. Make a face on the back side of the spoon with pieces of construction paper and glue on pieces of yarn for hair.

Paper Plate Bunny

Staple or sew together two paper plates around the edges leaving an opening at the bottom that is large enough for your child's hand to fit into. Cut long ears out of heavy white paper and attach with a stapler. Add features with a black felt-tipped marker or construction paper.

Stuffed Bag Puppet

Let your child make a face on the flat side of a paper bag using crayons or felt-tipped markers. She can then stuff the bag with newspaper and glue yarn pieces on top for hair. Insert a pole or stick at the bottom and tie around the bag with a heavy string.

Caterpillar

Cut a cardboard egg carton lengthwise and turn upside down. Pipe cleaners or a piece of wire may be poked through the front to serve as antennas. Features may be added with crayons, paint or felt-tipped markers.

Paper Bag Puppet

Use the flap of a small bag as the mouth for this puppet. Cut out two small triangles. Glue one triangle under the flap. Glue the other triangle on the flap. Both should be pointing down. Bend the top triangle up to form the puppet's mouth. Add construction paper, crayon or yarn features. Manipulate by placing hand inside bag and moving flap.

Stick Puppets

Select characters from a magazine. Let your child cut them out and paste to a tongue depressor or popsicle stick.

Potato Head Puppet

Almost anything can be used to make the face on this puppet . . . tiny marshmallows, cloves, paperclips, tacks or curled wire. His cap is made from the toe of a sock which has been turned up. Stick in a pencil at the bottom of the potato and he's all finished. Carrots, apples and turnips also make interesting puppets. Unfortunately, these puppets have a short life span.

Mitten Man

Tuck thumb of mitten inside. Add features of yarn and buttons. Manipulate by putting hand inside glove.

musical madness

Musical instruments are easy to make and even more fun to play. Invite in a few of your child's playmates and you've got an instant rhythm band . . . . You may decide, however, that this activity is best appreciated from another room!

Shakers

Fill bandage cans, spice cans, baking powder cans or cardboard tubes and boxes with rice, pebbles, beans or marbles and SHAKE, SHAKE, SHAKE.

Guitar

Stretch four or five rubber bands around a shoe box or cigar box. Pluck.

Chimes

Fill glasses with different levels of water and tap lightly on rim.

Humming Comb

Cover a comb with waxed paper and hum on the teeth of the comb.

Sand Blocks

Cut two pieces of 2.5 cm (1") thick wood about 5 cm x 10 cm (2" x 4"). Cut two smaller pieces about 2.5 cm x 5 cm (1" x 2"). Nail or screw the smaller piece onto the larger piece. Cut strips of sandpaper that are 7.5 cm x 13 cm (3" x 5"). Glue them onto the bottoms of the larger blocks. Scrape together.

Rhythm Sticks

Cut two pices of 12 mm (½") hardwood dowel about 23 cm (9") long. Hit together.

Horn

Blow gently into the top of an empty soda bottle.

Tambourine

Staple together two pie tins. Sew on bells or bottle caps or fill with small stones. Shake.

Cymbals

Strike two pan lids against one another.

Ringer

Suspend a fork, spoon or horseshoe from a string and tap lightly with a fork.

Coconut Clankers

Saw a coconut in half and clean out the inside. When the two halves are tapped together, they make an interesting galloping sound.

Rattles

Drill a hole through one end of a tongue depressor or popsicle stick. With a piece of wire, attach two or three bells to the stick. Shake. Instead of bells, you can also use bottle caps that have had a hole punched through the center with an ice pick. Attach to the stick with a wire.

Gong

Suspend a pot lid by a string and hit with a large metal spoon.

Drums

Stretch a piece of canvas, rubber tubing from an old tire or a thick piece of balloon across the top of a small barrel, a large coffee can or an oatmeal box. Secure by lacing, nailing or gluing to the side of the drum.

creating through art and music★★★★★

For the adult:

Bently, W. G., *Learning to Move and Moving to Learn* (New York: Citation Press, 1970). Excellent resource. Very moving!

Cobb, Vickie, *Arts and Crafts You Can Eat* (New York: Lippincott, 1972).

Kellogg, Rhoda, *Analyzing Children's Art* (Palo Alto: Mayfield Publishing Co., 1970). Traces the artistic development of children from two to eight, defining and classifying the forms common to children's art throughout the world.

Lowenfeld, V., *Your Child and His Art* (New York: Macmillan, 1965). A must to include on your reading list.

Proudzinski, John, *It's a Small, Small World But Larger Than You Think* (Washington, D.C.: Day Care & Child Development Council of America). A collection of songs, chants and movement activities to do with young children. Specifically designed for the nonmusician.

Rogers, Fred, *Mister Rogers' Songbook* (New York: Random House, 1970). Collection of favorite songs from the popular children's television show.

Tucker, Dorothy, *Foundations for Learning With Creative Art and Creative Movement* (Boston: Massachusetts Department of Mental Health, 1967).

Turner, G. Alan, *Creative Crafts for Everyone* (New York: Viking, 1959).

Young, Milton A., *Buttons Are to Push: Developing Your Child's Creativity* (New York: Pitman, 1970).

Sources of records for children:

(Write for catalogs)

Children's Music Center
2558 West Pico Boulevard
Los Angeles, Ca. 90019

Kimbo Educational Records
P.O. Box 246
Deal, New Jersey 07723

Folkways Records
165 West 46th Street
New York, New York 10036

Young People's Records, Inc.
100 Fifth Avenue
New York, New York 10011

what's cooking

There are many things your child can do in the kitchen that will not only instill valuable learning skills but will also be of help to you. S/he can help you scrub the potatoes, set the table, sift flour, grate or chop vegetables, pour milk from a pitcher, salt and pepper food, peel hard-boiled eggs and assist in making simple dishes. In fact, one of the fastest ways to get an uncooperative eater to eat more is to let him or her assist you in preparing the meal. The following recipes are included because they are tasty, nutritious and easy to make. It is up to you, however, to decide just how much assistance your child will need. Too much responsibility can be overwhelming, but be ready to allow your child to try new tasks. While you are in the kitchen together, talk about the taste, texture and color of different foods; this will make the experience far more meaningful and educational.

Cherry Milk

Add a few drops of cherry juice and one, two or three cherries to a glass of milk. Stir.

Colored Milk

Add a few drops of food coloring, 2 ml (½ tsp.) vanilla and 5 ml (1 tsp.) honey to a glass of milk. Stir.

Nutty Treat

800 ml (3¼ cups) oatmeal
240 ml (1 cup) unsweetened coconut
240 ml (1 cup) toasted wheat germ
240 ml (1 cup) favorite chopped nuts
  (like almonds or walnuts)
240 ml (1 cup) honey
60 ml (½ cup) melted butter

Preheat oven to 150° C. (300° F.). Combine oatmeal, coconut, wheat germ and nuts in a bowl. Heat honey and butter. Pour over dry ingredients. Spread on a cookie sheet. Toast in oven for 15-20 minutes.

Eggnog

2 eggs
30 ml (2 tbsp.) sugar
240 ml (1 cup) milk
2 ml (½ tsp.) vanilla
dash of nutmeg

Beat the egg with an egg beater until smooth. Add the remaining ingredients and beat until completely mixed.

Magic Eggs

3 slices bread
3 eggs
margarine
salt and pepper

Cut hole in middle of each bread slice with a 5 cm (2") biscuit cutter. On a hot grill fry each slice in one tablespoon margarine until golden brown. Turn. Slip egg into center of hole. Salt and pepper to taste. Fry about 3 minutes. Turn and fry 2 minutes until egg is done.

Applesauce

6 tart apples
120 ml (½ cup) sugar
360 ml (1½ cup) water
10 ml (2 tsp.) cinnamon

Peel, core and chop apples. Cook apples in water until tender. Add cinnamon and sugar. Mix well. Serve warm.

Chocolate Oatmeal Drops

30 ml (2 tbsp.) cocoa
60 ml (¼ cup) milk
240 ml (1 cup) sugar
240 ml (1 cup) quick-cooking oatmeal
60 ml (¼ cup) peanut butter
60 ml (¼ cup) margarine

Mix cocoa and milk. Stir in sugar and margarine. Heat until boiling for one minute. Remove from heat. Add oatmeal and peanut butter. Drop by teaspoonfuls onto waxed paper. Cool until firm.

Egg Salad

3 hard-boiled eggs
1 stalk celery
45 ml (3 tbsp.) sweet pickle relish
45 ml (3 tbsp.) mayonnaise
salt and pepper

Peel and mash eggs. Add the remaining ingredients. Serve on a piece of lettuce or spread on bread to make a sandwich.

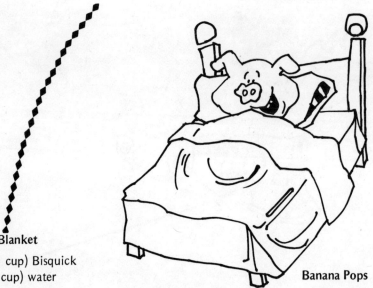

Pigs In a Blanket

240 ml (1 cup) Bisquick
60 ml (¼ cup) water
6 hot dogs

Mix Bisquick and water to form dough. Roll out into circle. Cut into six pie-shaped slices. Place hot dogs at wide end of each slice and roll up. Place on an un-greased cookie sheet and bake for 15 minutes at 230°C. (450°F.).

Cheesy Treats

120 ml (½ cup) shredded cheddar cheese
30 ml (2 tbsp.) onion
30 ml (2 tbsp.) mayonnaise
4 small slices of french bread

Set oven to 205°C. (400°F.). Mix all the ingredients. Spread on the slices of french bread. Bake for a few minutes until the cheese melts.

Sandwich Cut-Outs

With cookie cutters, cut out two pieces of bread the same shape for each sandwich. Spread soft cream cheese on one side and jelly on the other. Put the two pieces together.

Banana Pops

Peel three bananas. Cut each banana in half crosswise and insert a popsicle stick. Melt 120 ml (½ cup) semi-sweet chocolate chips (or butterscotch chips) and 5 ml (2 tsp.) margarine in a pan. Dip the banana into the chocolate and let cool. Yummy!

Potato Salad

800 ml (3¼ cups) cooked potatoes
1 onion
3 stalks celery
3 slices bacon, cooked until crispy
5 ml (1 tsp.) sugar
45 ml (3 tbsp.) sweet pickle relish
60 ml (¼ cup) mayonnaise
salt and pepper

Peel and cut potatoes into small cubes. Chop celery and onion. Crumble bacon. Put all the ingredients into a large bowl and toss lightly.

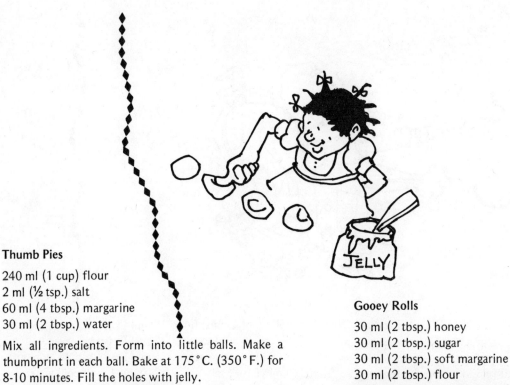

Thumb Pies

240 ml (1 cup) flour
2 ml (½ tsp.) salt
60 ml (4 tbsp.) margarine
30 ml (2 tbsp.) water

Mix all ingredients. Form into little balls. Make a thumbprint in each ball. Bake at 175°C. (350°F.) for 8-10 minutes. Fill the holes with jelly.

Gooey Rolls

30 ml (2 tbsp.) honey
30 ml (2 tbsp.) sugar
30 ml (2 tbsp.) soft margarine
30 ml (2 tbsp.) flour
1 package brown-and-serve rolls
1 small package nut halves (walnut or pecan)

Set oven to 190°C. (375°F.). Mix honey, sugar, margarine and flour in small bowl. Put rolls on baking sheet. Spread honey mixture on top of rolls. Arrange nut halves on top of the honey mixture. Bake about 15 minutes. Serve hot.

Popcorn

Use an electric popper or large saucepan. Let your child examine the kernels of corn before popping. Let him try to float a kernel before and after it has been popped. Make homemade butter to put on the popcorn.

Butter

Take 460 ml (1 pint) of heavy cream and pour it into a large jar. Screw on the lid and shake, shake, shake. Watch for lumps to form. Pour off the liquid (buttermilk) and add 1 ml (¼ tsp.) salt. Refrigerate. Serve on popcorn or spread on crackers.

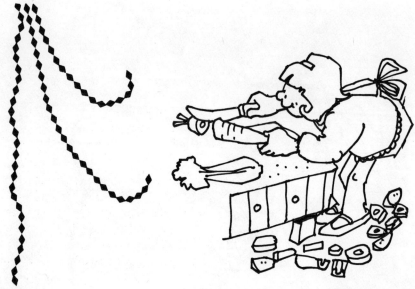

Fruit Salad

Let your child select five or six different fruits at the grocery store . . . like apples, peaches, pears, bananas, fresh pineapple or oranges. Peel and cut fruit. Put all fruit into a large bowl and fold in whipped cream or yogurt. Chill.

Alphabet Soup

2 cans stewed tomatoes
480 ml (2 cups) tomato juice
1 carrot, chopped
½ onion, chopped
1 small can of corn or peas
1 bay leaf
60 ml (¼ cup) alphabet soup noodles
salt, pepper and parsley

Put all ingredients into a large pot. Simmer for 1 hour.

Apple, Celery and Carrot Salad

5-6 apples (unpeeled)
2 stalks celery
1 carrot
45 ml (3 tbsp.) mayonnaise
salt and pepper

Chop apples and celery into small pieces. Grate carrot. Put into a large bowl and mix in mayonnaise, salt and pepper.

Crazy Cake

360 ml (1½ cups) flour	25 ml (5 tbsp.) oil
240 ml (1 cup) sugar	10 ml (2 tsp.) vinegar
45 ml (3 tbsp.) cocoa	5 ml (1 tsp.) vanilla
5 ml (1 tsp.) salt	240 ml (1 cup) cold water
5 ml (1 tsp.) soda	

Preheat oven to 175°C. (350°F.). Sift together flour, sugar, cocoa, salt and soda into an ungreased 20 cm (8") square pan. Make three holes in flour-cocoa mixture with the back of a spoon. Pour oil into the first hole, the vinegar into the second, and the vanilla into the third hole. Pour water over the mixture and stir well with a fork. Bake for 25-30 minutes. Cool on wire rack. Frost as desired.

Yumsicles

Pour your child's favorite fruit juice into paper cups and put in the freezer. When mixture gets mushy, stick in plastic spoons. Freeze. To eat, tear off cups.

Shake 'Em Up Bars

240 ml (1 cup) flour
7 ml (1½ tsp.) baking powder
2 ml (½ tsp.) salt
2 eggs
120 ml (½ cup) sugar
120 ml (½ cup) oil
120 ml (½ cup) orange juice

Preheat oven to 190°C. (375°F.). Grease a 23 x 30 cm (9" x 12") baking pan. Stir together flour, baking powder and salt. Set aside. Break each egg into small jar. Cover and shake 10 times. Add sugar, oil and orange juice. Shake about 20 times. Add flour mixture and shake until smooth. Pour batter into pan. Bake about 20-25 minutes. Cut into 12 bars.

Chicken Roll-Ups

480 ml (2 cups) Bisquick
120 ml (½ cup) water
1 can cream of chicken soup
480 ml (2 cups) diced cooked chicken
30 ml (2 tbsp.) chopped green pepper

Set oven at 230°C. (450°F.). Mix Bisquick and water to form dough. Roll out into a rectangle that is about 23 x 45 cm (9" x 18"). Mix 120 ml (½ cup) of the cream of chicken soup with the diced chicken and green peppers. Spread on the dough. Roll up along the wide edge and pinch edges to seal. Cut into slices and arrange in a greased baking pan. Bake 25-30 minutes. Heat the reamining chicken soup and use as a sauce over the chicken roll-ups.

goodbye

what's cooking •••

Children's Cookbooks

Bischell, Beth and Humphrey, Claudia, *Bake It Metric* (Oakland: Met-Cook Enterprises, 1975). The authors of this cookbook take the confusion out of metric conversion with simple metric recipes for tasty baked goods.

Cavin, Ruth, *1 Pinch of Sunshine, ½ Cup of Rain: Natural Food Recipes for Young People* (New York: Atheneum, 1973).

Croft, Karen, *The Good For Me Cookbook* (San Francisco: R & E Research Associates, 1971). Emphasis on healthful, nutritious recipes that cover a wide range of foods from different ethnic groups.

Ferreira, Nancy, *The Mother-Child Cookbook* (Menlo Park, Ca.: Pacific Coast Publishers, 1969). Focuses on the educational aspects of cooking projects for young children and the cognitive and social skills that can be gained through such experiences.

Goodwin, Mary, *Creative Food Experiences for Children* (Washington, D.C.: Center for Science in the Public Interest, 1974). An indispensable resource guide for nutrition education for young children. Well organized, thorough and very informative.

Parents' Nursery School, *Kids Are Natural Cooks* (Boston: Houghton Mifflin Company, 1974). Nutritious recipes with a sense of humor. Lively illustrations.

Petrich, Patricia, *The Kid's Cookbook* (Concord, Ca.: Nitty Gritty Books, 1973). An interesting collection of recipes that really appeal to children.

Wilms, Barbara, *Crunchy Bananas* (Salt Lake City: Sagamore Books, 1975).

TEACHER'S SUPPLEMENT

Dear Teacher,

Although **The Kids Do It Book** was originally written with the parent in mind, a quick look at its contents will show that it is also a valuable curriculum aid for any early childhood education program. Remember, however, that **The Kids Do It Book** was not designed to be followed activity by activity. Rather, it should be used by the creative teacher as a resource tool from which to draw, expand and generate new ideas tailored to the specific needs of his or her students.

In using a resource book such as this one, the teacher must always keep in mind that a child's learning is relative to the degree of involvement in the learning task. Involvement comes when activities are relevant and meaningful to each child's changing interests and developmental needs. The most important ingredient in this learning process is the child's self-image as a learner. If a child has repeated experiences in seeking, doing and achieving, then s/he will gradually derive a sense of self-esteem and a feeling of competence that breeds further success and motivation for future learning. The skillful teacher then will develop a curriculum that provides many learning experiences that nurture the child's emerging self-concept and foster self reliance.

One way this is accomplished is to key the curriculum to the seemingly insignificant day-to-day occurrences experienced by the child. For example, if a child in your class came to school with a bag full of old bones, a bird's egg or a dead worm, would you be flexible enough to jettison planned activities in favor of those that enhanced and amplified the child's new-found interest? What resources and activities would you be able to draw upon if the electricity went out in your classroom, if a spider walked across your path during storytime or if a child lost her first tooth during snack? The ways in which you are able to build upon such events and develop them into rewarding educational experiences will determine whether your students become active agents in their education or passive recipients of your teacher-directed tasks. **The Kids Do It Book** provides a framework for approaching each new incident, event or commonplace object that makes its way into your educational domain. Ask yourself in what ways the experience can be related to the different chapters on sensory awareness, reading readiness, math, science, art, music and cooking. Be inventive. Be spontaneous. And most of all, be flexible enough to drop an activity if it's going poorly. Obviously, such a curriculum means the end of the familiar teacher-lounge-boasting-game of "I have my lesson plans done for the next six months, how about YOU?" But the end of packaged deals and hidden agendas also means the end of apathy and disinterest. The teacher who generates a curriculum from the children's sparks of enthusiasm inevitably works harder and sleeps less not knowing exactly what to expect the following day. But the fire grows because a powerful message is conveyed to each child that s/he is an important individual whose thoughts, feelings and emotions are significant and worth-while. Such feelings enhance a child's self-image and cultivate curiosity and awareness of the world. Should the teacher of young children aim for anything less?

Another way that the skillful teacher fosters the child's self-concept is to weave a number of self-awareness activities into the curriculum. Because such activities appeal to the young child's egocentric nature, they help foster a better sense of self in relation to the external world. Described below are a number of activities that focus on self-awareness. Try to incorporate as many as possible into your curriculum. Because they center on the child's most personal world they will be both highly rewarding for the child as well as facilitate a healthy self-concept. Many are keyed to the pages of **The Kids Do It Book**.

ACTIVITIES THAT BUILD SELF-AWARENESS

1. The child's name. What is more personal than a child's name? Use it often! The following activities let the child know his or her name is important. Capitalize on this enthusiasm by instilling important cognitive skills of letter recognition and auditory discrimination as well.

First, middle, last name cards: (page 15)

Name rub: Drip white glue on a stiff card or small piece of cardboard to form the letters of each child's name. Let the glue dry for several days. Children will be able to magically make their name appear by laying a piece of paper over the name card and rubbing lightly with the flat side of a crayon.

Loony letters: (page 11)

Initial cards: Print each child's initials on a card (computer cards are good). These cards can be used to silently call roll or for a number of "match the card with the right child" games. You might also provide such a card for the children who cannot yet write their entire name. Instead of depending on the teacher to write their names on all their papers, such children can feel a degree of independence by being able to write one or all of their initials on their papers to identify their work.

Letter collage: (page 11)

Coil a letter: (page 10)

Rice name: Let the children spread glue on a piece of stiff paper or cardboard to form the letters of their name. Sprinkle rice on top (sand and cornmeal also work well) and shake off the excess. Many children will benefit from the opportunity to feel the shape of their name in addition to the visual stimuli.

Sandpaper letters: (page 10)

Alpha-bits cereal name collage: (page 10)

Hand talk: Clap out the syllables of each child's name with appropriate emphasis. Soon the children will be able to compare the beat patterns between different names.

2. **The child's concept of body.** The way in which children view and understand their bodies will have a great impact on their over-all self-image. The emphasis on the following activities should always be on the individuality of each child, not on how children compare with one another.

Mirrors, mirrors everywhere: Hang them high, hang them low. Tape expression cards next to mirrors of various shapes. Soon the children will be reading the words and acting out the appropriate expressions. Smile, frown, wink!

Self portrait: Have each child stand before a full-length mirror and examine different aspects of his or her body (eye color, shape of ears, nose, head, etc.). Then each child can color a self portrait keeping those details in mind. This is a good activity to do in September and again in June. Children can then compare the two pictures and note their progress.

Body talk: Play games that involve using the body instead of words to convey different thoughts. For example: "I'm tired," "Come here," "No."

Body word game: (page 13)

Body movement exercises: Movement activities that focus on different parts of the body and what each can do (go limp like spaghetti, stiff like a board, etc.) are excellent for instilling an awareness of self. Children can make different shapes or letters with their bodies working either separately or together in small groups. The possibilities for extending the child's imagination through movement activities are unlimited. Here are just a few:

  — pretend you're a marionette and someone is pulling your strings to make you dance, leap, fall, wave, etc.
  — pretend you're a bouncing ball, a rolling ball, a deflated ball.
  — pretend your arms are two magnets pulling at one another.

- pretend your head is made out of steel and is very, very heavy.
- pretend you're a bowl full of jello.
- pretend you're a rubber band being stretched.

Body puzzle: (page 13)

Preschool physiology 001: Let the children listen to their heart beat with a stethoscope. Stick out tongues at one another and examine each other's taste buds with small magnifying glasses. Demonstrate how knee reflexes work. Have the class lie down on the floor and have each child put one ear on another child's stomach to listen for a growl. Watch the pupil in a child's eye dilate when a flashlight is directed on it in a dark room (teacher controlled, of course). Examine hair, skin or fingernails under a microscope.

Silhouette cut-outs: Cast a child's shadow onto a piece of black construction paper. Trace around and cut out. Glue the silhouette to a larger piece of white paper. Makes a good gift for Valentine's Day.

Weigh and record: (page 24) Do periodically throughout the year. Record results and talk about growth.

Box people: (page 39) Make a whole class.

Photographs: Display photographs of the children engaged in different activities (enlargements are super if you can afford them). The children will be very eager to dictate stories about their friends. Type these dictations and attach to the photographs. The children will be able to read back their dictations in no time at all. Baby photographs are also excellent for prompting discussions about growth and development.

Tape recordings: Children are instantly captivated by the tape recorder. After their initial silliness in hearing themselves, the tape recorder can become a valuable tool, particularly for helping shy children express themselves more fluently.

Shadow play: (page 32)

Tempera footprints and handprints: (page 36)

Plaster of paris handprints: Mix plaster of paris according to directions on package. Grease a small pie tin with vaseline. Pour in the plaster of paris mixture and wait until semi-mushy. Press down on hand a few moments. Let dry and pop the mold out of the pie tin. Makes a great gift!

Feel it on your toes: (page 4)

Footprint numbers: (page 20)

Foot book: Trace around each child's foot several times. Let the child cut out the feet and attach together at the heel to form the pages of a book. The child can dictate a story about feet on the different pages. Make a cover and title "My Foot Book." Try also a book about hands or other body parts.

Back tracing: (page 11)

Fingerprints: (page 41) Or make a mixture of baking soda and carbon (available at hardware store). Spread the powder on a glass or dish that a child has handled. Brush off lightly to reveal fingerprints.

Action songs and routines: Songs like "Hokey Pokey" fingerplays or activity records that involve making the body respond to different cues and commands are good for instilling concepts of laterality and directionality. (Hap Palmer and Ella Jenkins put out some excellent records in this area.)

Stories and books about the body: For example: *Inside You & Me*, Eloise Turner, *Who Am I?*, June Behrens, *My Book About Me*, Dr. Suess and many many others.

3. The child's feelings and emotions. Teachers of early childhood education must strive to provide the kind of supportive atmosphere that encourages children to talk openly about their fears, wishes, fantasies and dreams. It is only when children begin to understand their vast array of emotions that they can begin to deal with associated behaviors in mature responsible ways.

Stories: Children are automatically drawn to stories that portray events and situations they can readily identify with. These stories can be used very effectively as a springboard for group discussions about different feelings and emotions. An example of some books that fall into this category are: *Feelings, Inside You and Outloud Too,* Barbara Kay Pollard, *Will I Have a Friend,* Miriam Cohen, *Lost & Found,* Kathryn Hitte, *It's Mine—A Greedy Book,* Crosby Bonsell, *Benjy's Blanket,* Myra B. Brown, *The Quarreling Book,* Charlotte Zolotow, *Ira Sleeps Over,* Bernard Waber.

Group discussions: If group discussions are conducted in a nonjudgmental, nonthreatening manner, children will openly share their thoughts and feelings with others. Some topics for discussion might be:

- more than anything else, I'm afraid of . . .
- I find it very hard to . . .
- I wish I could eat one million . . .
- my scariest dream was about . . .
- I wish that I could . . .
- I get very angry when . . .

Birthday celebrations: For the young child, a birthday is the most important day in the year. Yet some children are very perplexed why they don't somehow transform during that magical 24-hour period. Many good discussions can be generated from birthday feelings.

How do you feel? (page 14)

Dream pictures: Have the children color pictures and dictate stories to you about their dreams. These may be very insightful or completely misleading, so don't take them *too* seriously. Also read to the children *A Child's Book of Dreams* by Beatrice Schenk de Regniers.

Things I like and things I don't like: Countless projects for graphs, books and charts can be generated from the child's likes and dislikes. For example, "Foods I like," "My favorite television program," "My favorite wild beast," or "Things I can't live without."

"Dear Me" letters: Let the children write, dictate or scribble a letter to themselves. Address envelopes and mail to their respective homes.